OF CU BLESSINGS

A Poet's Dictionary of Humanity

A collection of poems by

Joseph L Bensinger

ISBN: 1516992636
ISBN 13: 9781516992638
Library of Congress Control Number: 2015913992
CreateSpace Independent Publishing Platform
North Charleston, South Carolina

For Twila, Jennifer, and Jesse,
who make me wiser
every day

PROLOGUE

When I wrote my first book, *Man, Ships, and the Sea*, it was just for fun and generally covered man's interaction with the ocean. Since its publication, and with my understanding of where I wanted to go with my writing, my next book, *Journeys through the Tapestry*, got more serious and covered a twofold purpose. For one, I wanted to introduce and share my feelings of the spirituality in nature, as with all things. Secondly, I wanted to meld some of the old nature religions with the concept of a single, multifaceted deity by reflecting and concentrating on a spirit of creation guided by love. In this new book, part of my intention is to define and delve into the character of man, good and bad, and explore the gift, or curse, of free will.

In Joseph Campbell's powerful video series, *The Power of Myth*, in conversation with Bill Moyers, he states that he thinks we need a new myth. That is, he feels that the religious documents of old are outdated in the sense that they answered the questions of a relatively primitive peoples but are lacking in the depth and understanding required to satisfy the curiosity of the more complicated, educated, modern world. Perhaps the new myth will be the second coming of the Jesus Christ of Christian tradition or some other personage of the past.

Or perhaps it may be something before, or different from, these foretold events.

Basically, we want more answers, have more questions, and want to know how it all gels with modern science. This book's objective, therefore, becomes twofold too—first, again, to explain man's free-choice options and, secondly, to start a discourse on what a new myth might explain in more detail.

If this book has caught your interest, I hope that you may be inspired to take the time to read the research and insight that inspired this writing. The concepts presented by the authors and books listed in the reference section have enormous consequences for the future of the human species. These concepts must be understood in order to create an enriched, sustainable, small planet with large human populations. An understanding of humanness, as the ancients knew, is critical to survival.

This may be nothing more than a dictionary of humanism, but it represents the partial culmination of thousands of years of written history dwelling on the contemplation and discourse concerning the thoughts and actions of man in regard to sins, virtues, and blessings.

CONTENTS

GENESIS

In the beginning was the Word,
and the Word was a thought,
and the thought instigated more
and felt loneliness.

Out of loneliness came self-compassion,
and from self-compassion came love—
that which is a unification
of the growing self.

Out of love came creation,
the Creator wishing to objectify,
for love is the foundation of creation.

IN THE BEGINNING

In the beginning there was a cause,
for without a cause
there is no beginning.
And, in the beginning was created
mass, space, and time.

So the cause must be that which is
outside of time.
That which has no time
has no beginning or end
but must lie in the realm
of the eternal.

That which requires no beginning or end
requires no cause and lies eternal.

LOVE

Some have found it in pain
others in loneliness,
and, yet, others
have always known it.

Love flows along on its own accord,
binding, yet unbound,
wild, and yet tame
and giving and taking of itself
in a path of its own choosing.

Yet love is but one kind,
and its grace supports your growth,
and its phases reflect
the growth of your heart.

Do not fear love
but accept the pain
of too much loving
so that you grow
to a new level of awareness
and know
of its grace and goodness.

Let even the hope of hope drive you
along love's manifest path—
along the golden rivers of your heart
toward the gleaming oceans of your soul.

For reason leads to love
as the voice of reason clamors
upon your heart for attention,
and the heart searches
the depths of your soul
for the Spirit's confirmation.
It chokes with compassion
at the longing for completion.

For when the heart touches the soul
a fullness is achieved
that exceeds all dimension,
as the soul is a fragment of
the Spirit that
envelopes all.

SIN[1]

Sin is the failure to see beauty
and express gratitude
for all creation.
Sin is a destroyer of creation
and a reaper of the chaos
from which creation came.

But for all the darkness
there is still the light,
and despair is not for those
who see with clear,
unblinded vision born
of the freedom of knowledge
and not confined by
the self-imposed ignorance
of failing to seek
and be curious, and searching.

For, in the quest, your identity is revealed
and your connection to the all, attained
and your eyes opened
in grace and compassion
and your joy, overwhelming
in the nurturance of the Spirit.

DECEIT

Oh, creature of the dark—
hidden, not to be discovered.
The light fades the desire,
and success becomes but a shadow
of its former self—the deceit
unveiled of its evil shroud.

Enlightened, the concealment is disclosed,
blanched of its former self-empowerment.
Wrought secrets illuminated in simple truths
reveal the smirching lie of fulfillment
by that which would guide
in loving kindness.

LOVE OF ANOTHER

You were made to have need of another
with passions, the depths to yet discover
in a true friendship that does not smother
but grows deep in pure love's breathing cover.

Let your passion for your beloved bathe free
in the warmth of the spring of truth and caring
and through the vapors let your soul's eye see
that your heart succumbs to selfless sharing.

Provide the space within yourself to listen
unto your heart's throbbing dance with your soul.
In a song of perfect kindness it will glisten
in knowledge of the oneness of the whole.

And, in an extension of self you mesh
in a release into one mind and flesh.

ENVY

Ruinous are your desires
to take from others
what you yourself do not possess.

Bitterness shall defeat you,
crush and consume you,
as you hate yourself for what you are not.

Brooding hate breeds self-hate
as comparisons abound
that measure worth and self-standing.

Take heed, envy, for love
is not something you possess
for the sake of yourself or others.

Better to love yourself
for what you are instead
of hating yourself for what you're not.

Better to go without
than deny the goods of others,
and destroy that which gives no satisfaction.

Better to seek the love
of the Spirit who made you,
and rejoice in finding your gifts.

Let your worthiness be
in the love of the Spirit
that bestowed you with the gift of life.

Let your desire be
to find contentment in reaching
the utmost of what you've been given.

DENIAL

Does the image in the mirror reflect the truth?
Does the view through the window portray reality
or negate the possibility?
Your heart knows your secrets,
and you conflict yourself
to your own discomfort.

The world is a dangerous place
in which to formulate illusions,
and fear does not resolve the complications
nor foster immunity.
You mock yourself with the desire
to create truth instead of
recognizing the possibility of hope.
Arrogance rationalizes lies
and creates a deception and barrier
to self-health and growth.

VANITY

When your gaze turns outward
do you not see the beauty in all things?
Would there be some merit in more or less?

Challenge the senses to see the whole—
Let the soul justify what cannot be questioned
and your consciousness ascend beyond yourself,
for in your mind's image you see only yourself
in a corruptible mirror of your own choosing.
But the mirror imparts a blind,
for it hides that which others may see
and feeds your own self-deception.
Arrogance and denial provide shallow satisfaction.

LOVE'S SACRIFICE[2]

That choice and commitment may stand the years
as gentle, daily feelings ebb and flow
will require a persistent compass that steers
in directions that hearts together grow.

Let not treason stand in the heartbeat's sway
as passion's tempests move past youthful storm
to tranquil relaxation in blessed play,
for loyalty spawns comfort's embracing form.

Rich, overflowing joy cannot be gained
that tide us over as harder times unfold
unless esteem shall reign, and fear is drained
in final defeat of vulnerabilities hold.

For love demands a never-ending action
in grateful strides of yet increasing traction.

SOUL'S PATH

Many, the years have I stumbled.
Many, the years have I crawled.
Now my heart is full blossomed
to the sway of my soul's great delight.

Many, the days have I wandered.
Many, the days have I searched
for meaning to base my life's path on
and the goals I would keep in my sight.

Many, the moments have I wondered.
Many, the moments have I mused.
But the Spirit has lit a bright pathway
and ended my wandering plight.

LOVE'S GRACE

As the moth seeks the light,
let your heart yearn for fullness.
As the moth scorches in the flame,
let your love burnish in the pyre.

Follow love wherever it finds you.
Seek its comfort and its pain.
When it beckons to you, reach out
and yield to its consummation.

When it speaks to you,
listen deeply to its message,
for the infinite is born of love
and all creation stands on its pillar.

IMPERFECT ME

Face all your imperfections with courage,
and let your self-compassion be the key
so that you can be loved for who you are
and not for what you want others to see.

You are one who has gifts and shortcomings.
You're one whose perfection will never be.
But, you are one whose long journey matters
because you chose to be falsity-free.

Hidden resources of your soul unfold
along the unseen ways, not yet foretold.

KNOWLEDGE

Engage your life as though following a trail
of knowledge in a journey of learning
and growth. Let love and commitment prevail
with steadfast aim, and persistent yearning.

We are well grounded in the reality
we choose ourselves to be surrounded with,
whether garnered from sweet spirituality
or hammered on the anvil by life's smith.

Cast back the blinding veil of deception
to a clear and honest awareness of self
based on a footwork of grounded perception
and by owning the story you penned yourself.

The trail of right direction has good ends,
but wrong turns face impenetrable bends.

LAUGHTER, SONG, AND DANCE³

Participate in the cosmic symphony
in any form you can accompany.

Laugh with the joy of the stories well told
in fellowship as life's journeys unfold.

Sing with the birds, for their freedom includes
flights through the heavens as their earth song exudes.

Dance with the wind for the wildness and beauty
of nature's whim in its creative duty.

And with creation's spirit you impart
joyful communication from the heart.

COURAGE[4]

Let not fear
control your life
but show courage
in doing what's right
with caution
in determining what may be
a reasonable response.

Do not be discouraged
by the few who do not
respect honesty
and forthrightness.

Showing vulnerability
is a kindness
to those
who would care.

ON LONENESS

Let your loneness
be the knife
that cuts the bonds
of your selfhood
and enlarges the presence
of your soul.

As ripples move
across the pond
so do souls reach
to the far beyond.

ALONENESS

You are never alone,
for there are those
that feel a connection
out of the darkness.

Those you don't know
who number with the stars
and know your presence.

Out of the darkness
of life's soup
radiates the blessing
of love's gentle kindness.

SORROW, SUFFERING, AND PAIN[5]

With the blessings
of free choice
in thought and action,
we know evil,
suffering and death.
This becomes
our training ground
for understanding and
a way to establish
some meaning in life.

You cannot live fully
until you have known
the good and the bad
the joy and the sorrow
of the wholeness of life.

In your fullness
you are connected, and
in your emptiness
you are filled larger
with the Spirit
that creates
the all.

And when you are filled
with the Spirit
being filled, you create
alongside the Creator
in the Creator's image
in the language of love,
expressed through
the heart,
which is the gift of gifts
shared among all
in gratitude,
grace, and beauty.

ON SORROW[6]

Let your mind suffer,
your body tire.
And in your poverty,
let the Spirit enrich you
as you were meant to be.
Let the place of sorrow
become renewed with hope,
for all love nurtures you
if you allow it to be.

ON SUFFERING[7]

In suffering
our pride is challenged
and emptied
of false security,
allowing room for the Spirit
to enter and fill us
with the joy and love
of shared connection.

In your suffering
let the Spirit show
you growth in meaning.

ON PAIN[8]

Pain defines you
as it is the crucible
that molds
your malleable self
in the fire of change,
a fire that
cannot be quenched
with suppressed apathy
or buried
in inflicted avoidance.

ANGER[9]

Consider the cost
of maintaining your anger
as it erodes
your health, for
the fire that is anger
eventually destroys all.

Learn to express
your feelings
and act with restraint
so that you may purge
the anger
and manage
a constructive
outcome.

Healthy anger
is a primitive force
that seeks an outlet
of empowerment,
but it must
in humility and gentleness
be enacted upon

and channeled into
a reasonable and justifiable
outcome.

Passions feed life
by sustaining
empowerment, justice,
perseverance, creativity,
kindness, and love.

CREATION[10]

Creation begets order from chaos,
and from order comes appreciation,
for the creation of further order
as the order identifies itself.

Indeed, what is the Spirit but order
that has identified itself? A self
that continually redefines itself
with the vast creation of more order.

Out of order comes our contemplation.
An imagination is born of this
that we nurture with love and compassion
in order that we may create and find
a universal connection with all
in bonded, intimate, shared awareness.

Life is animate creativity.

SEARCHING FOR JOY[11]

When we seek with our minds to know what we can
and strive among ourselves to understand
and wonder of other things beyond senses' span,
we come upon the infinite's helping hand.

In joy the inner soul is touched, as the heart
unfolds itself, removing the veil of blindness
so we see we are but a connected part
and seek the infinite's love in perfect kindness.

When we seek our creative selves and heed
the gift of imagination's soulful call
in intimate goodness our soul is freed
to join the infinite that creates the all.

But where there is no search, there is no repose,
for without spirit connection, fear may impose.

SORROW AND JOY[12]

In deep sorrow we may howl
as our minds screech out
from the winds
of our souls.

Yet even there
nature will revive us
with blessings
of kindness and love
and we will heal
if we allow the Spirit
to enter our minds
and touch our souls.

In your humility the soul is emptied,
and the Spirit will find
an even larger place to fill
with the joy of life's blessings
if you reach out
with the gratitude of connection.

You cannot live fully
until you have known
the good and the evil

and the joy and the sorrow
of the wholeness of life,
for in your fullness you are connected,
and in your emptiness you are filled larger
with the Spirit that
creates the all.

And the light of joy shall fill you
with hope and love.

GLUTTONY

Out of control—
the hunger pains
in promise of
happier times.

Obsessive cravings call
for immediate gratification,
as pleasure is centered
on appetite.
But fullness of stomach
is only temporary,
and the food of the stomach
is not necessarily,
the food that fills
the whole.

Helplessness is not
a necessary condition
for those who have
free choice
nor is food the remedy
for what ails
the heart and spirit.

LUST

Obsession feeds your desires
until addiction overwhelms the senses,
ensnaring you in self-serving interest
and creating a bond where none exists.

The voice of reason clamors upon
your heart for attention,
and your heart demands to give of itself
and take nothing.

Doomed is your harmony,
for mind and flesh are one
and cannot survive
in conflicted state.

Lost and empty, divorced from love
the fullness of promise
collapses to self-hatred
in the trapdoor of depression.

Pleasure is not necessarily fulfillment,
for it can be something sought
for its own sake
and not freely given.

Corruption of true human need
in the drink of self-absorption
creates a loneliness not quenched
and an intimacy not achieved.

In friendships are learned
an exchange of love's promise
in trust, unity, wholeness, respect,
goodness, and beauty.

BOREDOM/ACEDIA[13]

Despair eats at you
and loneliness becomes
your state.

Return to the sharing
and sociability
that connection requires,
as humans were not made
to be self-contained
but bolstered
in interdependent relationships.

COURAGE AND VULNERABILITY[14]

You don't need to be worthy
to take life's journey,
for the journey
makes you worthy.

And your worthiness
is not limited by your vulnerabilities
as you allow your courage
to claim
and capture them.

With courage
strength shall blossom
in your heart
while your soul
shall be your
forever companion.

Courage becomes
a kindness
to your selfhood
and rides above
criticism and fear.

Better to accept pain
than lack faithfulness
and commitment
to others
in false self-images.

HUMILITY[15]

An enlargement of self
that incorporates
the all
and recognizes
the shortcomings
of one who stands
alone.

It is
about having
an honest rapport
with all that surrounds you;
the courage to accept
your fragility, ignorance,
and mortality;
the responsibility
of honest self-appraisal
of your gifts and faults;
gratitude for the gifts
you have been bestowed.

It is about service
beyond self.

FORTITUDE[16]

Accept that there are
suffering and hardships
in life,
and see the worth
of these instances
as challenges to be endured
with a directed awareness
of the opportunity to learn
and develop a more wholeness
of self.

APATHY/SLOTH[17]

You fail to seek
new learning experiences,
and growth no longer occurs
because incapacitating indifference
exchanges boredom for motivation
and doing nothing
for doing what's right.

We become less than we are
unless life is pursued
with passion,
as loss of meaning
or purpose
induces a sadness
that sinks us to despair
and escapism.

You must remain committed
to seek your better self
and do that
which provides connection
to others
in kindness and love.

GRATITUDE

With joy and gratitude we oppose
the fears that life may bring
and accept the vulnerability
that the blessings of connectedness establish.

With courage we seek the Spirit's guidance
and, with courage, our souls and hearts dance
with the creative energies
of the universe.

Gratitude is a practice of freely giving
in humility, in return for something given.
It is an act of heart, a giving of feeling.
Yet, in action, it can be
as simple as a
"thank you."

KINDNESS AND COMPASSION

This well of kindness whose waters flow
with enduring patience
runs as a spring of gentle mirth,
for the gifts of life are
the Spirit's gifts of abundance,
which belies the strangeness of existence.

And what is true generosity
but a gift born of love
—a condition of the heart—
beyond all form of value,
which seeks no return
or attention.

How noble the gesture
that in our nature
we may do in kind
and in so doing, in turn
show value and respect
for all life
by understanding, helping,
and defending the vulnerable.

For such is the authentication
of compassion.

PRIDE/ARROGANCE

How false and superficial
the bubble may be
that surrounds you
if you deceive yourself
by bloating your importance
beyond honest introspection.

Pride can become excessive
to the point of
disordering our lives.
We can create self-images
that are shadows of the truth
and manufacture false happiness.

Righteous self-absorption
can also feed arrogance,
as denial obscures shortcomings
and makes you insensitive
and hard-hearted. For
arrogance breeds entitlement.

In honest reflection
you may see those things
that you might not prefer to see,

for when we acknowledge
our vulnerabilities and weaknesses
we see clearly
our false self-images
and the arrogance associated with them.
And see how the worth and power
are exaggerated
with feelings of superiority.

But denial of your shortcomings
does not serve you
any more than
denial of your gifts.
Success requires your strengths
and the strengths of others.
You, by yourself, are not sufficient,
for humankind was not made
to survive alone.

We long to be known
approved of
and part of something,
yet you distance yourself
from others
as they realize
the deceiving image you present.
All leads to loneliness
and isolation.

You have little control
over the events
in your life,
and happiness
is a matter of circumstance
not totally
in your control.
In humility and gratefulness
accept the contributions
of others.

PRIDE/SELF-LOVE

Let there be pride
in good choices, accomplishments
and the gifts given you
from the Spirit.

In honest appraisal
and self-acceptance,
self-love is just
and natural.

Accept yourself
for what you are,
and treat yourself
with kindness and compassion.
Love does not require worthiness
for all are worthy as they are
without reservation, conditions,
approval, or acceptance.

With self-love you will not fear
to bring the true you to the fore
And only with the real you
will you get a true sense
of belonging
to the all.

GREED

Your desires may control you
with no limit
if you become a slave
to possessions.

You seek happiness
but may find misery,
for though you may be blessed
with material wealth,
excessive desire for material things
may stunt your desire
and devalue those things
of true human value.

Contentment may not be yours
if you do not know
what you truly need
to be satisfied.

Seek those things
that satisfy the heart
and create inner joy.
Let compassion rule your heart
before greed turns you
to treachery and deceit.

As you have been blessed
with the richness of material things
so also can you be blessed
with the happiness and joy
of your compassion, kindness,
and generosity.

WRATH

In courage
let your anger
seek the goodness
to make things right.

Pause to reflect
as patience
calms and cleanses
the mind and heart.

Without self-centered action,
reason may prevail
and your judgment clear
as to what is good and just.

LANDSCAPE

The symbiosis of all
is beyond our simple minds,
but that does not make it less except
in our perceptions.
We are, perhaps, left
with a feeling of ordered chaos.
But, in fact,
it is an artwork—
the artwork of creation.
It is a reflection of
the personality of the Maker
and is well beyond
the mere artifice
of human construct.

A creation of the past
and the present. An ongoing process
transforming before our eyes and minds
that is forever in fervor
adding, changing, modifying,
and redesigning itself.
A process that makes time meaningless.

The excitement is palpable,
the possibilities, mystical.
The Spirit is vibrant and alive.
In love, it creates
and has no further purpose.

THE CHOICE

Although his life grows tired and weary,
and though his life grows short,
he reflects upon his many blessings,
although he's fallen short.

He reflects upon the loves he's had
and the few he's left behind,
and in the causes won or lost
and the tolls upon his mind.

He looks upon a wave-filled beach
and the wavelets cast by sea
as though God's fingers reach to touch
in fellowship sent free.

The trees and plants well speak to him
on the gentle earth's fresh breath
—the leaves' and needles' calm whispering
concerning life and death.

The mountains yawn and speak to him
in their majesty and might
of the firmament of creation's blaze
and of eternal night.

And the flaw that gave us freedom's voice
thus born of Eden's fall
presents a course of eternal fate
beyond death's final thrall.

And then he looked upon earth's throne
where mortal man does stand
and was shaken to his very bones
and strove to understand,

He saw that man had failed to serve
the many needs that call
but only served himself, at best
but little else at all.

He saw with pain man's character flaws
that free will sorely brought.
The ability for reason dims
where intelligence is naught.

That which leads to self-destruction
are sins of thought and deed
that lead to disordered lives because
they limit the will, once freed.

For the blessing of free will provide
the power to clearly see
that responsibility; self-control
will make us truly free.

But he saw something greater than us
beyond ignorance and bliss
and came by faith there was a guide
to forgive us when amiss.

Life cannot be trivial and trifling
nor loneliness absolute.
If we have hope, and faith, and love
the trunk grows from the root.

REFERENCES

DeYoung, Rebecca Konyndyk. *Glittering Vices: A New Look at the Seven Deadly Sins and their Remedies.* Grand Rapids: Brazos Press, 2009.

Sullender, R. Scott. *Ancient Sins...Modern Addictions: A Fresh Look at the Seven Deadly Sins.* Eugene: Cascade Books, 2013.

Brown, Brene. *The Gifts of Imperfection: Let Go of Who You Think You're Supposed to Be and Embrace Who You Are.* Center City: Hazelden, 2010.

Keller, Timothy. *Walking with God through Pain and Suffering.* New York: Dutton, 2013.

Fox, Matthew. *Sins of the Spirit, Blessings of the Flesh: Lessons for Transforming Evil in Soul and Society.* New York: Three Rivers Press, 1999.

------------------. *Creativity: Where the Divine and the Human Meet.* New York: Penguin, 2004.

Schimmel, Soloman. *The Seven Deadly Sins: Jewish, Christian, and Classical Reflections on Human Psychology.* Oxford: Oxford University Press, 1997.

ENDNOTES

1 Inspired by *Sins of the Spirit, Blessings of the Flesh*, p. 124–127.
2 Inspired by *Glittering Vices*, p. 97, and *The Gifts of Imperfection*, p. 77–85.
3 Inspired by *Creativity*, p. 47–55, and *The Gifts of Imperfection*, p. 117–124.
4 Inspired by *Glittering Vices*, p. 148, and *The Gifts of Imperfection*, p. 7–15.
5 Inspired by *Creativity*, p. 45–47, and the book *Walking with God through Pain and Suffering.*
6 Ibid.
7 Ibid.
8 Ibid.
9 Inspired by *Sins of the Spirit, Blessings of the Flesh*, p. 234–237.
10 Inspired by the book *Creativity.*
11 Inspired by *Sins of the Spirit, Blessings of the Flesh*, p. 268.
12 Inspired by *The Gifts of Imperfection*, p. 77–85.
13 Inspired by *Sins of the Spirit, Blessings of the Flesh*, p. 167.
14 An excellent discussion can be found in *The Gifts of Imperfection.*

15 Of particular note is the discussion in *The Seven Deadly Sins*, p. 39–54.
16 For a more complete description of fortitude, see *Ancient Sins...Modern Addictions*, p. 103.
17 Inspired by *Ancient Sins...Modern Addictions*, p. 84–95.

CPSIA information can be obtained at www.ICGtesting.com
Printed in the USA
LVOW10s2108120716

496032LV00025B/485/P